Sarah Johnson Everett

History of the Baptist Church at Stoke Green

Sarah Johnson Everett

History of the Baptist Church at Stoke Green

ISBN/EAN: 9783743326347

Manufactured in Europe, USA, Canada, Australia, Japa

Cover: Foto ©ninafisch / pixelio.de

Manufactured and distributed by brebook publishing software
(www.brebook.com)

Sarah Johnson Everett

History of the Baptist Church at Stoke Green

HISTORY

OF THE

BAPTIST CHURCH

AT

STOKE GREEN, IPSWICH,

COMPILED FROM AUTHENTIC RECORDS,

BY

SARAH JOHNSON EVERETT.

FOR PRIVATE CIRCULATION ONLY.

COWELL'S STEAM PRINTING WORKS, IPSWICH.

1871.

HISTORY OF THE BAPTIST CHURCH,

STOKE GREEN, IPSWICH.

CHAPTER I.

THE Baptist Church now assembling at Stoke Green is one of the oldest in the county of Suffolk; Bildeston alone shows an earlier date. At the time when these Churches were formed, there was scarcely an evangelical minister to be found in the Established Church, and spirituality was at a very low ebb. Dissenters were looked upon as such disloyal and dissatisfied people, that it was dangerous and disgraceful to have any connection with them. Their meetings were subject to violent interruption, the ministers and hearers occasionally fined in heavy sums, as may be seen in the history of the Church at Diss, or in the Life of Mr. John Thompson, of Culpho; and the Government treated them as disloyal subjects, sometimes calling upon them to take the oath of allegiance.* It is very

---

* The compiler of this little work holds the Certificate that one of her family did, as a Dissenter, in 1723, at Bury St. Edmund's, take the oaths appointed in the first year of the reign of His Majesty George the First, for the security of his person and government.

difficult for us now, enjoying so large a measure of religious liberty, to realize the position in which dissenters then stood.

The Churches at Stoke and Bildeston were both, originally, branch stations of the Church at Eld Lane, Colchester, which was formed a year after the Revolution. There is an entry in the Colchester Church Book, dated October 29, 1729, directing " Brother Rootsey (the minister) to go to Woolverstone, to break bread to that branch, for their furtherance and spiritual growth, once a quarter." Again we find that Mr. Richard Starting (who died in 1752, and was assistant to Mr. Dunthorne, Mr. Rootsey's successor), supplied when needful, at Colchester, Langham, and Woolverstone. The same records show that, November 2, 1757, nine men and four women desired and obtained leave to unite with the Church under the pastoral care of Mr. Samuel Sowden; and the earliest records of the Church at Stoke Green show that on the 22nd of November, 1757, a Baptist Church was formed in the village of Woolverstone by eight men and four women, and at the same time Joseph Sage and Stephen Bruce were chosen deacons.

In April, 1758, they invited Samuel Sowden to become their pastor. As his name in the old list stands directly after the names of the twelve original members, it is possible that he was the ninth man mentioned as dismissed from Colchester,* though not formally chosen minister till a few months later. Mr.

---

* That Mr. Sowden came to us from Essex appears the more probable, as Mrs. Sowden, after his death, was dismissed to Langham, another branch of the Church at Eld Lane.

Sowden came originally from Cannon Street, Birmingham. He preached in a little house on the Berners' estate, and used to baptise at the Cat House; the grandmother of the late Archdeacon Berners used to go, and she preserved for them the greatest order and decorum; almost the greatest kindness she could have shown them.

After a lapse of fifteen years and a half, Mr. Sowden died; the place of meeting was taken from them, and they were thus placed in difficulty. The Church had increased considerably in numbers, but our knowledge of their proceedings is small, as no regular minutes of their meetings during this time are recorded. They had, April 6, 1761, unanimously sent one of their number forth to preach the Gospel, John Hitchcock, who preached at Wattisham; and in October of the same year, "did, by solemn fasting and prayer, set apart two of the brethren, Wincoll Grimwood and Isaac Johnson, to the sacred office of Deacons." A family used to come from Ipswich, and one from Claydon, and they considered whether they should make an effort to stay at Woolverstone, or remove to Ipswich. A piece of ground was thought of between the Rose Inn and the present Turret Green Chapel, in Ipswich, and was partly engaged, but the Woolverstone friends were too strong to allow it. Stoke was ultimately decided on. From the present Pastor's house to the road was a row of cottages; the house nearest to the road was used as a vestry, a Chapel was made of the centre cottages, and the house at the other end was set apart for the minister. The frontage to the road was originally much longer than it now is, for it included the ground now occupied by Messrs. Hunt and Harvey; but in July, 1812, the church " agreed to dispose of a piece of land, containing thirty rods or thereabouts, on which a building has lately been erected, and is now in the occupation of Widow Hall and others; and that the money for which the above said piece of land should be sold shall be applied to the use of the estate."

The license to use the buildings for religious worship was obtained November 27, 1773, in the Registry Office of the Bishop of Norwich.

CHAPTER II.

WHEN the church was formed at Woolverstone, it consisted of only 12 members, but by the time it removed to Stoke it had increased to 44.

In the spring of 1775 the Rev. George Hall became the pastor; the congregation then was small, and they were able to raise barely £50 per annum, but from this time they increased rapidly in numbers and usefulness. The records of their proceedings were, from this time, regularly kept; and we learn that though the public services were held at Stoke, the church meetings were still frequently held at Woolverstone, generally at the house of Mr. Thomas Ridley, occasionally at that of Mr. Last; and when there were candidates for baptism, the church, after the meeting, adjourned to the Orwell, and there baptised. Then for a time the church meetings were held "at Mrs. Sage's, at Freston Tower," (a farm house adjoining, now pulled down,) and the candidates were baptised "in the Orwell, at Freston Brook," till in 1799 a baptistry was made on the premises at Stoke, in the yard adjoining, and friends who can remember it, tell us it looked like a grave.

One record in the old book shows us the different state of opinion in religious matters one hundred years ago to that of our own time. In April 1777, the Baptist Ministers of the Quarterly Association having been consulted on the case of a country brother, gave their opinion that "catching wild fowl on the Sabbath is neither a work of necessity or of mercy." What church in Suffolk now would think of referring such a question to the Association?

In December, 1779, the church, at Mr. Hall's suggestion, chose a deaconess, Mrs. Johnson. We are not told what her duties were, nor was the office filled up, when after a few years she removed to Woodbridge, where she died suddenly, sitting by the fire side, and was buried in the Chapel in Cutting's Lane, now called Beaumont's Chapel, after the name of its founder, a French refugee, to whom she was related.

In 1781, the church was £30 in debt for necessary expenses and repairs, and agreed to write to the neighbouring churches at Colchester and Wattisham, praying their assistance; they replied they were not able to assist us.

In 1784, another gifted brother was called to the ministry, Mr. Thomas Ridley. He had been chosen a deacon four years before, and after his call to preach he assisted Mr. Hall in various ways, often taking his place in baptising, till in 1798 or 9 he removed to Bury, and became the first pastor of the church there, now under the care of the Rev. C. Elven.

In 1798, forty-three members were dismissed to form a church at Grundisburgh, under the pastoral care of Mr. John Thompson one of our gifted brethren, who was instrumental in raising other churches in this county. Mr. Thompson's extensive usefulness demands more than a passing notice ; his history, too, shows so clearly the religious state of the county at that time, that a sketch of him here cannot be considered out of place.

He was born near Bury St. Edmund's, in 1755, and early prided himself on the strict discharge of all his moral and religious duties. Naturally of a generous disposition, his charity to the poor was his chief reliance for acceptance with God. A conversation with a pious shoemaker directed his attention to the doctrine of salvation by faith in Christ, and led him to search the Scriptures. "Faith came by the word, and for nearly fifty years he built his hopes of divine mercy, and acceptance with God through a mediator, seeking forgiveness through the kindness and love of God our Saviour, experienced by the washing of regeneration and the renewing of the Holy Ghost by faith." He was, at this time, a strict churchman, but was unable to find a church, where the gospel was preached either to his satisfaction or edification. He revolted at the idea of entering a dissenting place of worship, but at length he was persuaded to attend a prayer meeting, and what he heard and witnessed was congenial with his views and feelings, yet he thought that the church was the place where men ought to worship, and that to forsake it, was a sin against God and the State. He felt as if he had rather lose his life than be prevented attending where he might hear the gospel, and resolved to attend every church for miles round, even going as far as Colchester, but all in vain; and this was, at first, his only motive for becoming a dissenter.

He joined the church at Stoke, in 1780; this provoked persecution from his own and his wife's parents, and they expressed their determination to disown him if he persisted in attending with dissenters. He answered their threats in the pathetic language of Scripture, "When my father and mother forsake me, then the Lord will take me up." This so touched his own dear mother that falling on his neck, and with a flood of tears she repeated again and again, "My dear, I will never forsake you; Oh! no, you shall never be forsaken." From that time the storm of persecution in a measure subsided, though his friends never acquiesced in his becoming a dissenter.

The church at Stoke chose him deacon in 1784, and such was the confidence both minister and people reposed in him, that for ten years he was the only acting deacon. For several years before he became a minister, he was very usefully employed in expounding the Scriptures from house to house, where people met for prayer and reading the word. Mr. Keeble, late of Blandford Street Chapel, London, dated his conversion to him when thus employed, and he was useful to many others. The success of these labours of love induced the church to request him to exercise his gifts with a view to the public ministry, and in 1796 they gave him "full liberty to exercise his gifts and preach the gospel where God in his providence should call him." This call the Great Head of the church abundantly sanctioned, and opened for him an effectual door at Grundisburgh, a village two miles distant from his own residence, Culpho Hall.

In July, 1798, a church of forty-two members was formed there, and he was unanimously chosen pastor. He was favoured with respect in an eminent degree in his own country, collected a congregation of 800 persons, and his labours were owned and blessed in a pre-eminent and remarkable manner. During his ministry he baptised and added to the church 658 persons, also assisted in planting in the neighbourhood four additional churches, viz., Otley, Tunstall, Charsfield, and Sutton; he esteemed it an honour to spend and be spent for Christ.

Many now living have heard their parents speak of the riots that attended the efforts he made, along with others, to introduce the gospel to Wickham Market. The first meeting which was held, September, 1810, was interrupted by a riotous mob of nearly one thousand persons, and at every fresh attempt to hold services the mob assembled in greater numbers and with increasing violence, till their conduct became so outrageous that bills of Indictment were preferred against the ringleaders at the Woodbridge Quarter Sessions, but the Grand Jury ignored the bills. The mob, therefore, took fresh courage, and when the Rev. Matthew Wilks, unable to believe the reports that had reached him, of the lawless conduct of the rioters, went himself to preach, the interruption was so violent that the congregation was obliged to disperse. The protection of the Court of King's Bench was next applied for, in February, 1811. The Court granted a Rule to show cause against six persons, who, to disentangle themselves from this Rule, pleaded guilty, and paid the sum of two hundred guineas, and entered into recognizances to keep the peace for ever.

This and other acts of illiberality, induced some gentlemen of different denominations to form " The Protestant Society for the Protection of Religious Liberty." This society paid the costs of the law proceedings in this case, and presented the two hundred guineas to the Suffolk Auxiliary British and Foreign Bible Society, on condition that the inhabitants of Wickham Market should always be well supplied with Bibles and Testaments.

Mr. Thompson continued his ministerial labours till within two sabbaths of his death ; his last public service being the administration of the Lord's Supper. He died October 9, 1829, in the 71st year of his age, and the 30th of his ministry. Not less than 1500 people assembled to hear the funeral sermon, which was preached by his friend, Mr. A. K. Cowell, from whose published account of Mr. Thompson's life and labours this sketch has been taken.

CHAPTER III.

The year after Mr. Thompson had been sent out to preach, that is, in 1797, the church at Stoke called to the work of the ministry Mr. John Keeble, who was afterwards the minister of Blandford Street Chapel, London ; and in December, 1798, Mr. James Fenn, and Mr. A. K. Cowell were called to preach. The former preached at Otley ; Mr. Cowell for several years assisted Mr. Hall at Stoke, baptising most of the candidates after Mr. Ridley removed to Bury, and as Mr. Hall's health failed, he performed gratuitously all the work of the pastor. He was afterwards for many years pastor of the church at Walton, which was formed in 1808 by the dismissal of 38 members from Stoke, and was at first under the care of Mr. Making.

In 1800, Mr. Thomas Hoddy, afterwards of Clare, was called to the ministry; and three years later, Mr. James Smith, who became pastor of the church at Ilford, making the seventh member called to preach during Mr. Hall's ministry.

In 1809, messengers to candidates for baptism are first named, the candidate not being generally known; previously to this, candidates appear to have been proposed, and, if approved of, immediately called in to relate their experience; and two years later it was agreed that, before any person came to relate their experience, they should speak to the minister, and he should inform the church of their intention.

Mr. Hall died in February, 1810, after having been pastor of the church for 35 years, and having seen it grow from the 44 members he found at the commencement of his ministry, to 230 at its close. He was born in York, removed to London when about 18, and in 1770 joined the Baptist Church in Unicorn Yard, then under the care of Rev. W. Clarke. The church soon recognised his gifts, and in 1773 sent him forth to preach the gospel where God in his providence might open a door. In two years he removed to Ipswich, where he became deeply loved and esteemed for his piety, prudence, and zeal. He excelled as a pastor, visiting from house to house; he also found many friends of different denominations, amongst whom was a worthy clergyman in the neighbourhood, the Rev. Michael Marlow who interested himself very much, and in a practical way, in his welfare. God abundantly blessed his efforts, for during the 35 years of his pastorate 424 persons were baptised.

During the first half of his ministry there were several unpleasant dissensions in the church, but his peaceable disposition and advice served considerably to quench the coals of growing strife, and in the first seventeen years he was at Stoke he baptised 92 persons. About the year 1792 there was a revival in the church, and from that time to Mr. Hall's death in 1810, 337 persons were baptised, and the chapel twice enlarged.

For five months previous to his death, Mr. Hall endured a very severe and trying affliction. His people often visited him, and some of his conversations with them have been preserved. " Satan has been trying to disturb my peace, but I feel satisfied that I shall not be sent to hell, because I have been thinking it is not from want of disposition, but from want of strength, that I am not preaching Christ ; and if I die with a disposition to preach Christ, if I were sent to hell, I should preach him there, and such a subject would not suit that place."

He gave directions respecting his funeral, saying he was not concerned where he should be buried ; but recollecting the circumstance of a minister who said, when he was dying, that his people had trodden upon him all his life, therefore he would be buried at the meeting door, that they might trample upon him when he was dead, Mr. Hall added, " My people have not trodden upon me in my life, therefore I should not like to be buried at the meeting-door, to be trampled upon when I am dead." He died February 26, 1810, aged 64, and was buried in the chapel by the Rev. Jabez Brown, of Stowmarket.

CHAPTER IV.

IMMEDIATELY after Mr. Hall's death, a letter was received from Mr. Shenstone, a Baptist Minister in London, recommending Mr. White as "a sound, savoury and experimental preacher," and in his opinion likely to suit our Church well. As Mr. Cowell objected to take the entire pastorate, Mr. White was invited, and was, with his wife, received from Ashford, Kent, in August of the same year, 1810. During his short pastorate of less than four years, forty persons were added to the church, and in March, 1813, the church agreed to become members of the Baptist Missionary Society. Mr. White resigned at Midsummer, 1814, but appears to have remained unsettled for some time; for in February, 1819, he and his wife were dismissed to Lowestoft.

For more than a year the church remained without a pastor, till, in October, 1815, Mr. Payne accepted the invitation of the church, and removed to Ipswich from Newport, Isle of Wight. Out of the six ministers who took part in his recognition services, four were formerly members of the church at Stoke, and by it were sent out to preach; viz., Mr. Thompson, of Grundisburgh; Mr. Cowell, of Walton; Mr. Keeble, of London; and Mr. James Smith, of Ilford. Mr. Jabez Brown, of Stowmarket, and Mr. Weare, of Salem Chapel, Ipswich, also took part in the services.

About this time there is occasional mention of other Baptist Churches in the town, not now in existence. One was in Long Lane, and we are told it was originally occupied by the Wesleyans, before they built the chapel in New Market Lane; another was in Dove Yard, and a third is spoken of as the " General Baptist Church," in Orwell Street.

We obtain an amusing insight into their social services by the following record : " May, 1824. Agreed, at our prayer meetings a portion of Scripture to be read, to sing shorter, and pray shorter, that a greater number may engage." A note in the margin of the book adds, " The person who made this proposition reduced his prayer to thirty-five minutes, as an example."

In May, 1825, thirty persons were dismissed to form a church at Chelmondiston, where Mr. Isaac Double preached. He was a member of the church at Stoke, called to the ministry in June, 1824, and was brother of Jeremiah Double, many years a respected deacon.

In October, 1826, Mr. Payne resigned, after a ministry of twelve years, during which time nearly 200 were baptised and added to the church, our late pastor, Mr. Webb, among the number; a considerable part of them came from surrounding villages. Mr. Payne's preaching was eminently experimental. In 1827, he removed to Ashford, in Kent, and there having been for some time completely broken down in health, he died about 1850.

His removal was partly caused by the outbreak of a grievous heresy, which began with a curate who preached in this town, and was considered evangelical. He began by finding fault with the doctrine of the Trinity as incomprehensible, and went on step by step, many following him, until they denied the doctrine of justification by faith in Christ, and landed at last in something like practical infidelity. Most of the churches in this town were infected, and he soon left the Church of England.

While the church was without a pastor, the pulpit was supplied for some time by the Rev. Isaiah Birt.

In October, 1827, six members were dismissed to form a church at Somersham.

CHAPTER V.

In May, 1828, Mr. Sprigg accepted the invitation to the pastoral office. He was sent out by the same church which Mr. Sowden left, but came to Ipswich from Ireland. Twenty members were dismissed the following January to form a church in Bethesda Chapel, which was then closed, but had at one time been occupied by the Independents.

In January, 1830, a room in Union Street, Cox Lane, was engaged for evening services, and this was exchanged three years and a half later for one in Tacket Street, in which the Sunday evening and week evening services continued to be held for several years after Mr. Webb came.

The church at Stoke took a warm interest in the Abolition of Slavery. In 1830, resolutions against Slavery were passed at a church meeting, and in January, 1833, a day was appointed as a day of prayer with reference to the state of affairs in the West Indies. The Independent congregations also observed the day, and by the suggestion of Tacket Street friends, the evening service was a united prayer meeting of the three congregations, held in Tacket Street Chapel, and many still living can remember the interest felt in Mr. Knibb, and the warm sympathy he met with on his visits to Ipswich, to advocate the cause of freedom.

In February of the same year, 1833, the church

unanimously agreed to request Mr. Samuel H. Cowell to supply the pulpit at Stoke on Sabbath afternoons during the summer, and he often rendered similar services in later years; sometimes, through the winter, conducting the Sunday evening service in the vestry at Stoke, during the pastorate of Mr. Webb, while the latter was preaching in the room at Tacket Street.

In March, 1835, twelve members were dismissed to form a church at Framsden; and in June of the same year, nineteen were dismissed to form a church at Crowfield.

In 1838, the question of moving into the town was first mooted, and was revived at intervals, till in April, 1842, Mr. Sprigg resigned, and was accompanied by forty-five members to form a church in the town, now the Turret.

During the fourteen years of his ministry, about 300 were added to the church, and we have the testimony of our venerated friend, Mr. Pollard, that " From Mr. Sprigg's ministry great results followed. He had seen more than we had, and introduced a better and sounder system of church government than we had before known. He was a beloved and useful minister." After preaching some years at the Turret, Mr. Sprigg became pastor of the Baptist Church at Margate, then of that at Westbury Leigh, and died in Australia in 1868.

For nearly a year the church at Stoke remained without a pastor, the pulpit being supplied in the summer by Mr. Ierson and Mr. Haycroft; they were then students whose college course was not completed, and both have since become leading men, though in widely different religious bodies.

CHAPTER VI.

In February, 1843, Mr. Webb of Arnsby, Leicestershire, began his labours among us; recommended as suitable by Messrs. Aldis and Elven. Mr. Middleditch, late of Salem, took the afternoon service for the summer. The same year the vestries were rebuilt, the original cottage vestry having been left standing till that time ; two years later the old cottage parsonage was pulled down, and the present modern house erected. The vestries were not enlarged to their present size till 1862. The same year that the new house was built, a fresh appointment of Trustees was made. The following minute was recorded in the church book, a fitting tribute to a generous friend : "March 31, 1845. The church here records its affectionate and grateful memorial of its late much esteemed friend, Mr. A. K. Cowell, and of the valuable gratuitous services rendered by him in former years in conducting the public worship in this place ; and on these grounds resolves, that the Secretary of the Incidental Committee be directed to charge the Burial Fees the same only as for our own members.

In February, 1850, a tea meeting was held to commemorate Mr. Pollard's having been a member fifty years, during the greater part of which time he had honourably and usefully sustained the office of deacon.

He was a native of Debenham, removed to Ipswich

when about twenty-three, and at first, often attended the ministry of the late Mr. Atkinson, at Tacket Street, and there is good reason to believe that by it he was led to find peace in the Saviour. He joined the church at Stoke, in February, 1800, being baptised by Mr. Cowell, and six years after was appointed a deacon. By industry and care he managed to acquire a little property, and about the year 1800 he entered into the malting and corn trade, and for many years he was successful. But about 1833 he sustained heavy losses, owing in part to the great fluctuations of the corn trade. No one sustained injury from his losses, but his own little property was entirely swept away. The sympathy and respect felt for him was shown by his friends rallying round him; two of them, especially, affording him such important aid, that he was enabled to resume his business as a corn merchant. His domestic life, too, was often clouded. On his wedding day, a sister of his bride was also married, but though in usual health in the morning, in the evening of the day death claimed her for his victim. Young people may be interested in finding out her grave, which is near that of our friend Mr. Pollard, and there they may read her name, Mrs. Cooper, and her affecting story. Mrs. Pollard survived her sister more than forty years, but her children were all removed in early life; the last, in 1835, by lingering consumption.

Mr. Pollard was especially interested in the Foreign Mission, and on account of important services rendered to it, he was for many years placed on the list of the Committee as an honorary member. In his old age he was pre-eminently the friend of the young; he had always a kind word for them, they were welcomed to his home, he would find them suitable work in connection with the church, and if he saw young believers hesitating to profess their faith in Jesus, he would encourage them to come forward. Though in feeble health, he was in his usual place the sabbath before his death, which occurred rather unexpectedly at the last, at an early hour on Sunday, August 28, 1853, in the 84th year of his age.

Six years later, a brother deacon who had worked with him for many years, Jeremiah Double, was called away. Baptised in 1802 by Mr. Cowell, he, like Mr. Pollard, was a member of the church at Stoke for more than fifty years. Though only a farm labourer, he was a beloved and respected deacon for thirty years. In social life he could only speak with difficulty, his stammering being a great hindrance in conversation, but in the worship of God he was able to speak plainly; would conduct a prayer meeting, read a hymn and lead the tune, read a chapter, expounding it with useful remarks, and pray for twenty minutes without any hesitation.

Towards the close of 1862, the chapel was altered, and the vestries were re-built in their present form; and in the following January the upper vestry was the scene of the sudden death of our beloved deacon, Mr. William Root. He was received at Stoke from Harwich in 1822, and was chosen a deacon in 1829, at the same time as Jeremiah Double and Mr. G. Bayley, now of Camberwell. For a time he gave out the hymns and led the singing, but gave up that office to Mr. Neve, in 1833. He was pre-eminently the friend of the poor and afflicted. He attended the prayer meeting on Monday evening, January 12, 1863, apparently in his usual health, and was called on by Mr. Webb to engage in prayer. After he had offered several petitions, his voice suddenly dropped to a whisper ; he fell, and all efforts to restore consciousness were vain ; and, though it was felt that such an instant exchange of prayer for praise was a happy escape from the terrors of death, yet the solemn feeling that death was actually present at the meeting, will never be forgotten by any who were there.

October 7, 1866, Mr. Webb preached his last sermons as our pastor. After preaching for some time in London, he became co-pastor of a Baptist Church at Bury, in Lancashire, and tutor at Chambers Hall College, near that town. While he was at Stoke, 565 were added to the church, and at one time the number of members stood as high as 380.

CHAPTER VII.

August 1, 1867, Mr. Osborne preached his first sermon as pastor, and during his stay of three years, 67 were added to the church. The year after he came, that is, in 1868, died Mr. Robert Lacey, who for more than fifty years held the office of deacon. He was born at Trunch, in Norfolk, in December, 1787, removed to Bury St. Edmund's at the age of 19, and a few months after was led to serious reflection by the death of a young lady to whom he was engaged. He thought, Oh! if I had been taken instead of her, where should I have been? The old deacons of the Baptist Church at Bury noticed him, but at first he drew back from any open profession of religion, afraid of saying more than he felt; but at length he was encouraged to come forward, and was baptised by Mr. Cole, at that time minister of the church. Mr. Lacey remained at Bury between two and three years, and then removed to Ipswich, where he joined the church at Stoke, just before Mr. Hall's death in February, 1810.

After a short residence in Ipswich, he was preparing to take a business and have a home of his own, when a second time death blighted his hopes; the lady died after a short illness, and he resolved to continue in the employment in which he then was. He was among the first teachers in the Sunday School, and though his religious principles sometimes annoyed his master, yet they so far won his respect that orders were given that he should always have his dinner as soon as he wished on Sundays, whether his employer was ready or not.

In 1812 he married the widow of Mr. David Everett; in 1816 was chosen a deacon of the church at Stoke, and for 52 years he served the church with a lively interest, ever striving for its peace and prosperity. For eighty years he enjoyed unbroken health, but for a few months before his death he suffered from a peculiarly trying affliction, which gradually removed the power of speech. He died in May, 1868.

Mr. Osborne concluded his ministry at Stoke,

October 30, 1870, and early in the following year became the pastor of Stepney Chapel, Lynn.

January 1, 1871, Mr. Whale, of Bures, preached his first sermon as pastor of the church at Stoke.

———————

Cowell's Steam Printing Works, Ipswich.

www.ingramcontent.com/pod-product-compliance
Lightning Source LLC
Chambersburg PA
CBHW031156090426
42738CB00008B/1356